CRAFT TOPICS

STUARTS

FACTS ● THINGS TO MAKE ● ACTIVITIES

RACHEL WRIGHT

Photography by Chris Fairclough

Watts Books

London ● New York ● Sydney

© 1993 Watts Books

Watts Books
96 Leonard Street
London EC2A 4RH

Franklin Watts
14 Mars Road
Lane Cove
NSW 2066

UK ISBN: 0 7496 1139 1

10 9 8 7 6 5 4 3 2 1

Editor: Hazel Poole
Designer: Sally Boothroyd
Consultants: Dr. A Hassell-Smith,
                Rosemary Harden
Photographs by: Chris Fairclough
Artwork by: Ed Dovey

A CIP catalogue record for this book is available
from the British Library

Printed in the United Kingdom

CONTENTS

THE EARLY STUARTS 1603-1642

The age of the Stuarts began in 1603 when Queen Elizabeth I died and her cousin, James Stuart, King of Scotland, became King James I of England.

James's accession to the English throne united the crowns of Scotland and England, but that was as far as union went. Although he wanted his two kingdoms to share the same laws, government and Church, the English wouldn't accept this. Their ancient rivalry with the Scots ran deep and they were not prepared to join forces with their poorer northern neighbours. It wasn't until 1707 that both countries were united under one Parliament and James's dream largely came true.

RELIGION, REBELLION AND PLOT

Religion played a very important part in people's lives under the Stuarts. Everyone was expected to go to church regularly and many were willing to risk their lives for their religious beliefs.

During the Middle Ages, Roman Catholicism had been the religion of western Europe. But in the early 1500s many people became critical of Catholicism and started to form their own churches instead. These people were known as Protestants.

◀ *James I of England (and VI of Scotland) was a member of the Stuart royal family. He reigned over England, Scotland, Ireland and Wales from 1603-1625.*

In 1611, James I ordered a new English translation of the Bible. This version of the Bible is still available today.

By the beginning of James's reign, most people in England were Protestant. Not surprisingly, English Catholics were far from thrilled about this. But, except for a few failed attempts to overthrow James in the early 1600s, most of them settled down under their new king and put up with the restrictions imposed upon them.

Extremist Protestants, nicknamed Puritans, also became less troublesome under James. During Elizabeth I's reign, Parliament had declared that the practices of the Church of England should be a mixture of Protestant and Catholic ideas. Unlike most Protestants, the Puritans were not happy with this. They wanted to stamp out all traces of Catholicism from the Church. When it became clear that James would agree to some of their reforms, many of them stopped challenging the Church. Those who were not so happy packed their bags and from 1620 onwards left England to settle in North America.

▲ The most dangerous conspiracy of James's reign took place in 1605, when a group of Catholics tried to blow up the King and the Houses of Parliament. Every year, on November 5, the English celebrate the defeat of this plot. Bonfires are lit throughout the country and, in some places, a straw figure of Guy Fawkes, one of the leading conspirators, is burned.

▼ The Puritans believed in simple worship and plain living.

EMPIRE BUILDING

The Puritans who left England in 1620 were neither the first nor the last to settle abroad under the Stuarts. In 1607, English settlers founded a colony in Virginia, North America, and from 1630 onwards ship-loads of people left their homes to settle along North America's east coast. Later on, settlements and trading posts were also set up in Canada, the West Indies, India and the Far East. From these beginnings the British Empire was built.

PERFECT TIMING

The early 1600s were ideal for Empire building because England was more peaceful than she had been for a long time. Improvements to English ship-building and navigation, which had begun in Elizabeth I's reign, also made it safer to travel far and wide.

None of these transatlantic trips would have been possible, however, had they not been financed by wealthy London merchants. By providing would-be settlers with ships and funds, the merchants hoped to set up permanent colonies where they could trade English goods, for example woollen cloth, for American products such as cotton and tobacco.

◀ The first group which set sail for America in 1620 were known as the Pilgrim Fathers. Over 100 of them made the voyage aboard a 6 metre wide and 27 metre long trading ship called The Mayflower. Ask some friends to help you mark out these measurements in your local park. You'll soon see just how cramped conditions on board ship must have been.

IN SEARCH OF THE GOOD LIFE

Not all colonists went abroad for religious reasons. Many were farmers and craftsmen who simply wanted to own land or find work.

All these settlers were well suited to life in an unexplored land. Most of them had grown up in small communities which either grew or made nearly everything that they needed. As a result, they all knew how to build their own houses, grow their own food and make their own clothes.

Most English people were also used to running their own local affairs, which was a great help when it came to setting up colonies. Although King and Parliament made the laws of the land, they relied on powerful landowners to make sure that these laws were obeyed. In turn, each landowner relied on his tenants and local villagers to police their own communities and check that everything ran smoothly.

▼ As in England, farming in the colonies was carried out with simple tools and no machinery. The Pilgrim Fathers were helped in their fields by a native American called Squanto, who showed them how to plant corn.

KING AND PARLIAMENT

In early Stuart times, Parliament was much less powerful than it is today. As long as a monarch gained the consent of his Members of Parliament (MPs) before introducing new laws or taxes, he could govern without their advice.

Ruling without the support of Parliament was not always a good idea, though, as James's son, Charles I, discovered. In 1629, after a series of arguments over his disastrous foreign policy, Charles decided to dismiss Parliament and rule without them.

▶ Charles I succeeded his father, James I in 1625 and died in 1649.

Did you know that the nursery rhyme "Humpty Dumpty" dates back to the Civil War? It celebrates the collapse of the Tower of Humpty in Essex.

▼ Those who fought for the monarchy and the Church of England were called Royalists or Cavaliers. Those who fought for Puritanism and Parliamentary rule were called Parliamentarians or Roundheads. They were given the nickname "Roundheads" because of their short hair and round helmets.

At first Charles's "personal rule" went well. But in 1637 he tried to make religious worship in Scotland more like that in England. Enraged by this meddling in their affairs, the Scots rebelled and in 1640 they invaded England.

Charles knew that the only way to get rid of the Scots was to make a treaty with them. But to do this he needed parliamentary approval, and so in November 1640 Parliament was reinstated.

Once summoned, MPs began to argue with the King about how the country should be governed, and how much power the King should have. These arguments got more and more heated, and by 1642 the King and his opponents were ready for war.

THE CIVIL WAR AND BEYOND

The Civil War, which lasted for seven years, was eventually won by Parliament's army, and on 30 January 1649 Charles I was executed.

With the king dead, Parliament ruled Britain as a republic. This meant that those who were elected to Parliament decided how the country should be governed. But quarrels amongst MPs and rebellions at home and abroad soon threatened chaos. To meet the crisis, the army's leader, Oliver Cromwell, took charge and from 1653 he ruled as a military dictator.

Under his energetic leadership, the army and navy restored order at home and boosted Britain's image abroad. Yet, despite Cromwell's successes, his rule became unpopular. As a strict Puritan, Cromwell believed in hard work and simple living. He had no time for "sinful" pleasures such as gambling, going to the theatre or eating Christmas dinner – all of which he banned. These restrictions put a lot of people off Puritanism for good!

▲ Oliver Cromwell's statue stands outside the Houses of Parliament in London. It celebrates his achievements as a great Parliamentarian.

THE RESTORATION OF THE MONARCHY

Despite the high hopes that many people had for the republic, it did not last. When Cromwell died in 1658, quarrels broke out among rival generals in Parliament's army. Without a strong leader to calm the growing chaos, a number of MPs decided that the only solution was to restore the monarchy. So, they invited Charles I's eldest son to return to England as King Charles II.

PAPER CROWNS, PASTE JEWELS

▶ *After the execution of Charles I, Parliament sold or destroyed all the royal jewels, including the crown Charles had worn for his coronation. When Charles II came to the throne a new crown was made, which is still used for coronations today.*

You will need: a sheet of thin gold card • scissors • sticky tape • tape measure • glue • paste jewels, beads or shiny gummed shapes • a strip of velvet, wide enough to fit around your head with about 2cm to spare, and long enough to cover your head from your eyebrows • a strip of cotton wool, the same length as the width of the velvet • scraps of black felt • needle and thread.

TO MAKE THE VELVET CAP

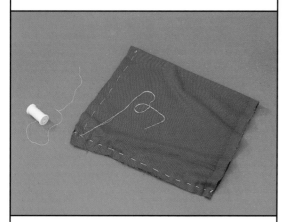

▲1. Sew the ends of the velvet together to form a tube, and then sew a line of running stitches across the top. Make sure that the softer side of the material is on the inside of the tube.

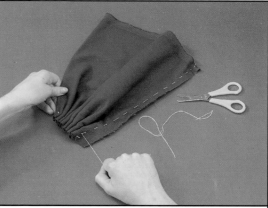

▲2. Pull the thread at the top of the tube and tie a knot in it.

3. Turn the cap inside out. Dab some glue around the bottom of it and stick the strip of cotton wool into place. To make this trim look like ermine, add little flecks of black felt.

TO MAKE THE FRAME OF THE CROWN

4. Put the cap on your head and ask a friend to measure around the top edge of the cotton wool. Cut out a strip of gold card the same length as this measurement, and tape the ends together to form a headband.

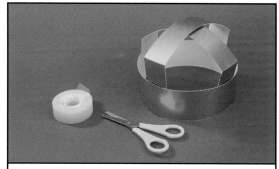

▲**5.** Cut two more strips of card, long enough to reach over the top of your head from one side of the headband to the other. Tape the strips to the inside of the headband and fold them slightly, as shown.

TO MAKE THE TOP OF THE CROWN

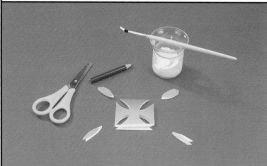

▲**6.** Fold a rectangle of card in half. Mark and cut it as shown. Glue the two crosses together and stick their tabs onto the top of the crown.

TO DECORATE THE CROWN

7. Glue card crosses and other shapes to the inside of the headband and decorate the whole crown with paste jewels, beads or shiny gummed shapes.

To become king or queen for a day, put on the velvet cap and slide the crown over it.

11

THE MERRY MONARCH

When Charles II arrived in London in May 1660 he was greeted by crowds of cheering supporters. After the rules and regulations of the Puritan era, the people of England hoped that Charles would liven things up a little. And this he did. He forgave most of his father's enemies, restored the Church of England, re-opened the theatres, and acknowledged the power of Parliament.

In fact it was Parliament, not the King, which proved the less forgiving. Charles wanted to extend his tolerance to all religious groups. But Parliament, which was now packed with Church of England royalists, refused. Instead it insisted that those who would not accept the teachings of the Church of England should be penalised and barred from holding positions of power.

CULTURED KING

Like his father, Charles II was a cultured man. Throughout his reign he always encouraged art, drama, and music. He also employed a talented architect called Christopher Wren to restore his palaces, and a team of gardeners to smarten up the royal parks. His example was quickly followed by others and throughout the country, wealthy landowners started re-designing parks and rebuilding their war-torn homes.

◄ Charles II ruled from 1660-1685. Although a married man, he had lots of love affairs, none of which were very secret!

THE AGE OF SCIENCE

Charles II also encouraged science, and it was during his reign that the famous science club, the Royal Society, was founded.

Before the 1600s, most Europeans had explained natural happenings in religious terms: stormy weather meant that God was angry with the world. Sunshine was a sign that He was pleased. Members of the Royal Society challenged this way of thinking. Through experiments, exact measurement and calculation they sought a more scientific explanation about how the universe works. Their discoveries in astronomy, physics and mathematics, together with those made by other European researchers, laid the foundations for modern science.

THE COLOUR OF LIGHT

Newton proved that white light is made up of an assortment of colours. He did this by directing a beam of sunlight through a narrow slit onto a triangular prism of glass.

▲ *The most brilliant member of the Royal Society was Sir Isaac Newton (1642-1727). Among other things, he explained the laws of gravity, and made important discoveries about the nature of light.*

You will need: a round glass of water • a piece of card with a vertical slit in it, about 1 cm wide • a piece of white paper • sticky tape • a sunny day!

1. Tape the card to the glass, as shown. Now stand the glass on the paper, by a window, and watch what happens when a beam of sunlight passes through the slit in the card.

As the sun's light passes through the slit it is bent, or refracted, by the water in the glass. This enables you to see some of the colours that make up sunlight as they re-emerge from the water.

Ribbons and Lace

After his father's execution, Charles II had fled to France to the court of the flamboyant French king, Louis XIV. Under Louis, the French court was the most elegant in Europe, and when Charles returned to England he brought with him a taste for fine French fashion. Out went the plain outfits of the Puritan era and in came more colourful clothes, decorated with masses of braid, ribbons and lace. English fashion followers became so crazy about ribbons that they virtually covered themselves in them. According to records of the time, one pair of trousers had no fewer than 250 yards of ribbon sewn into it in bunches!

The frills and finery of the rich were not shared by the poor, many of whom had only one or two hard-wearing outfits. Many ordinary people wove their own cloth and made their own simple clothes at home. These clothes were usually made from wool, because sheep were plentiful.

Woollen cloth was England's biggest export. Weavers up and down the land made the cloth in their own cottages, and then sold it to men who worked for wealthy merchants.

WIGS AND PATCHES

From Charles II's reign onwards, all fashionable men wore curly wigs, even soldiers. Imagine charging into battle with a mass of artificial hair stuck on your head!

You will need: a swimming cap • PVA glue • strips of black paper of different widths and lengths.

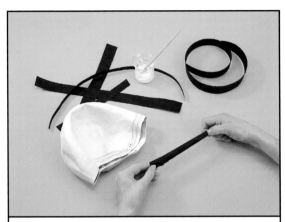

▲1. Twist or roll the strips of paper into ringlets and curls and glue them onto the swimming cap. (If the swimming cap has a bumpy outer surface, turn it inside out first).

Women didn't usually wear wigs during the late 1600s, but they did wear face patches. These patches, which were cut out of black cloth, were designed to decorate the face – and cover up spots!

You will need: black cloth • a teaspoon of flour • two teaspoons of water • scissors.

1. Cut shapes, such as crescents and stars, out of the cloth. Mix the flour and water into a paste and use it to stick the shapes onto your face.

THE GREAT PLAGUE

In the hot, dry summer of 1665, London was hit by a terrible disease called the Plague. Thousands of people fell into a fever, developed black lumps and died.

With so many victims dying every day, it was vital to bury the dead quickly. Carts were sent clattering round the cobbled streets each night to collect the dead bodies and take them to huge burial pits. Sometimes the pain of the plague was so unbearable that sufferers threw themselves into these pits of their own accord.

FLEAS AND DISEASE

The plague was not a new disease. The earliest outbreak, called the Black Death, had swept through Europe in the 1300s killing millions of people.

The main reason this deadly disease was so common long ago was that no-one understood the link between dirt, germs and illness. Everyone threw their rubbish and sewage out into the street and few people bothered to clean their homes or have a bath. As a result, towns swarmed with rats, and just about

everyone had fleas. Had the Stuarts or their ancestors known, as we do, that the plague was spread by rat fleas, things might have been different. However, since they had no idea that filth and fleas were the cause of all their troubles, they continued to live under the threat of disease.

KILL OR CURE

Like the rest of the population, doctors had no idea what to do about the plague. The only thing they did know was that they didn't want to catch it themselves! So they dressed in long leather robes, broad-brimmed hats, gloves and hoods.

The hoods had eyeholes made of glass and a bird-like beak, stuffed with herbs. Imagine how the poor patients must have felt when they saw this coming towards them!

The Great Plague turned London into a ghost town. Those who could fled to the country. Others shut themselves in their homes.

Red crosses were painted on house doors where the plague had struck, to warn passers-by.

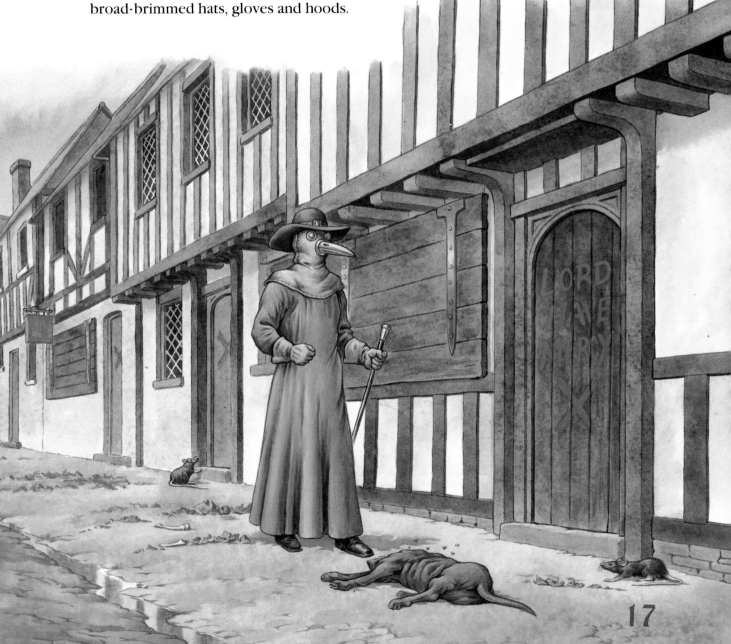

THE GREAT FIRE

By the spring of 1666, the plague had died down and everyone, including the King, returned to London.

Six months later, however, disaster struck again. A bakery in Pudding Lane caught fire and set light to the entire street. Before long, the whole City was ablaze and Londoners were once more forced to flee for their lives.

The fire, which raged for four days spread quickly because most of the capital's houses were made of wood and positioned close together. The City's hand-operated fire engines were not capable of tackling a blaze of this size, and it was only when the strong wind fanning the flames dropped, that the fire eventually went out.

▶ *Christopher Wren (1632-1723) was responsible for rebuilding many London churches, including St. Paul's Cathedral. Like James I's architect, Inigo Jones (1573-1652), Wren was heavily influenced by the classical architecture of ancient Greece and Rome.*

Six days after the fire had ended, the architect Christopher Wren offered a revolutionary plan to rebuild London in a more structured way. Sadly this plan wasn't adopted because most people wanted to rebuild their homes where they had been before. Yet, despite this London was improved. Many streets were paved and widened and a number of buildings were rebuilt in brick or stone.

FEATHER WRITING

One of the reasons why we know so much about the Great Plague and the Fire of London is because a Londoner called Samuel Pepys recorded these events in his diary. Like other writers of that time, Pepys wrote with a quill pen and ink.

You will need: a large, dry feather (a turkey feather would be ideal) • a small sharp knife • a hard cutting board • a needle • a small paintbrush • ink • paper.

Ask an adult to help you as the knife will be very sharp.

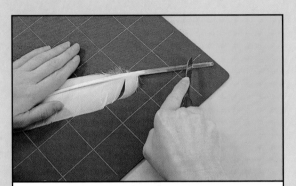

▲ **1.** Put the feather, top side down, on the cutting board, and carefully make a slightly curved cut into its shaft. You need to start the cut about 3 cm from the tip of the feather and continue in a straight line towards the tip.

▲ **2.** Now make two slightly curved cuts, either side of the tip. These cuts should be parallel and slope down to the tip.

3. If the inside of the shaft isn't clean and hollow, clean it out with a needle.

▲ **4.** Place the feather on the cutting board and cut a straight line across its tip. Hold your knife at a slight slant as you do this.

▲ **5.** Cut a small slit into the middle of the tip, as well. This will help the ink to flow more easily.

6. Now brush a little ink onto the back of your quill's nib and start scribbling! Try not to press too hard and don't be put off by the scratching noise your pen makes!

PLAYS, MUSIC AND POETRY

OFF TO THE THEATRE

During the early 1600s everyone, from courtiers to common people, flocked to London's theatres to see all kinds of plays, including the works of William Shakespeare, the greatest playwright of all.

▶ *An Elizabethan theatre. The wealthy sat on the stage itself or in the covered galleries around the theatre's walls. Poorer people sat or stood in the pit in front of the stage.*

Like the Elizabethans before them, the early Stuarts loved plays that were packed with shocks, surprises, jokes and disguises. They joined in the action whenever they could, and often hurled food and insults at the players if they didn't think the acting was good enough.

When London's theatres re-opened after Cromwell's rule, their plays reflected the mood of Charles II's court. Witty, mocking and rude, these plays were written for the fashionable rich and staged in smaller, more elegant theatres.

In many ways these changes did more harm than good. Prices increased, which meant that only the rich could afford them, and the immoral nature of the plays lowered the theatre's reputation. All this had a terrible effect on the stage and from the late Stuart period, English theatre was no longer taken as seriously as it had once been.

◀ *Judging by the huge number of plays to his name, William Shakespeare (1564-1616) must have been an incredibly fast writer. It is said that one of his plays,* The Merry Wives of Windsor, *was written in just two weeks flat!*

A CHANGE OF TUNE

The Puritans were not noted for their support of the arts, but it was under Cromwell that the first English opera was composed. This is not as surprising as it seems, though. Singing and playing musical instruments were popular family pastimes throughout the Stuart period, even under the Puritans.

Charles II's composer Henry Purcell also wrote an opera, the famous *Dido and Aeneas*. Blending Italian and French styles with traditional English music, Purcell composed pieces for stage, Church and Court. His music is still enjoyed today, and many people regard him the greatest native-born English composer.

MEN OF LETTERS

The 1600s produced some excellent English literature. In addition to the works of William Shakespeare, the Stuart Age enjoyed the hilarious plays of Ben Jonson, the majestic poetry of John Milton and the witty verses of John Dryden.

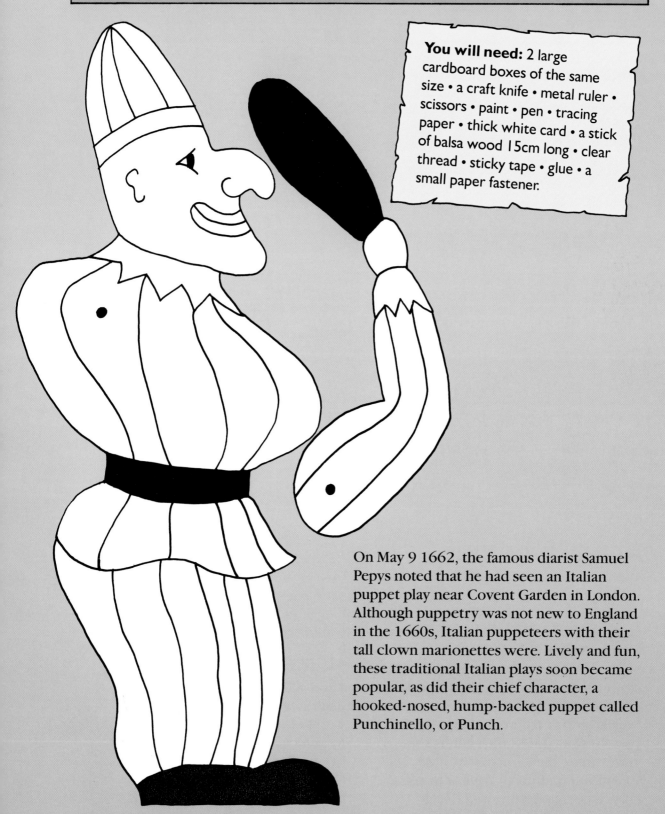

You will need: 2 large cardboard boxes of the same size • a craft knife • metal ruler • scissors • paint • pen • tracing paper • thick white card • a stick of balsa wood 15cm long • clear thread • sticky tape • glue • a small paper fastener.

On May 9 1662, the famous diarist Samuel Pepys noted that he had seen an Italian puppet play near Covent Garden in London. Although puppetry was not new to England in the 1660s, Italian puppeteers with their tall clown marionettes were. Lively and fun, these traditional Italian plays soon became popular, as did their chief character, a hooked-nosed, hump-backed puppet called Punchinello, or Punch.

Ask a grown up to help you as the craft knife will be sharp.

TO MAKE THE PUPPET THEATRE

▲ **1.** Cut a stage opening into one of the cardboard boxes.

▲ **2.** Draw identical diagonal lines on opposite sides of the second box and cut along both lines. Now cut along the top and bottom edges of the box where they meet the diagonal lines.

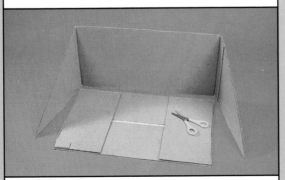

▲ **3.** Cut away the bottom of one half of the box. You should end up with a triple-sided piece of card.

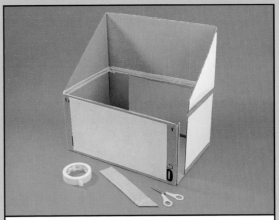

▲ **4.** Tape the triple-sided piece of card to the top of the first box. Cut a stage entrance, about 6cm wide, into one of the side walls and paint the whole theatre, inside and out.

TO MAKE MR PUNCH

5. Trace the shapes on page 22 onto some tracing paper. Copy the tracings onto the white card and cut them out. You'll need to copy the larger tracing twice.

▲ **6.** Paint both sides of the arm cut-out and opposite sides of the two body cut-outs, as shown.

7. Ask an adult to make a small hole near the top of the arm cut-out. Make a hole in one of the body cut-outs as well, and join the two pieces together with the paper fastener. Pull the arm away from the body slightly before you tighten the paper fastener, and check that it moves easily.

23

8. Tape a length of thread to the back of Mr Punch's head, hump and chest. Lower his arm and tape some thread to the back of his hand, as well.

▲**9.** Ask a friend to hold Mr Punch upright and steady while you tie the threads to the stick of balsa wood. Wind each thread around the stick first and only knot them when Mr Punch hangs straight. (Red thread has been used here to show clearly what is meant.)

▲**10.** Glue both sides of Mr Punch together and hold him upright by the balsa support. If you find it hard to steady him, glue a small oval of cardboard to his feet and paint it.

11. Mr Punch is now ready for action! You can either hold the balsa support and make him float just above the stage floor or you can pull his hand string up and down to make him look menacing.

THE GLORIOUS REVOLUTION

Charles II and his wife had no children, so when Charles died in 1685, his brother became King James II. James was a firm Catholic and once crowned, he set about trying to lift the restrictions imposed upon his Catholic subjects. Although this led to conflict with Parliament and the Church, they both put up with James because he had no male heir. This meant that when he died his grown-up Protestant daughter, Mary, would inherit the throne and reverse his pro-Catholic policies. Imagine everyone's shock, therefore, when on 10 June 1688 James's wife gave birth to a son and Catholic heir!

James II reigned from 1685 to 1688.

The prospect of another Catholic king filled many with horror, and shortly after the birth, seven leading statesmen asked Mary's Protestant husband, William, ruler of Holland, to come and save the nation. Anxious to add England's wealth to that of his beloved Holland, William accepted the offer. But James's and William's armies never met. Within weeks of his son-in-law's invasion, James fell ill and fled to France, leaving his throne open for William and Mary.

◄ *Many Protestants didn't believe that James II's son was the Queen's child. They thought that he was an abandoned baby who had been smuggled into the royal bed.*

25

CONFLICT IN IRELAND

James II was not prepared to give up his throne without a fight and in 1689 he went to Ireland to raise an army. Although many Irish Catholics supported James, his army was no match for William's, and after losing the Battle of the Boyne in 1690, James returned to France.

The Battle of the Boyne was not the first time that the Catholic majority in Ireland had suffered at Protestant hands. Like Elizabeth before him, James I had increased his authority in Ireland by encouraging Scottish and English Protestants to settle there. Although Irish Catholics were outraged by this, it soon became clear that there was little they could do to stop a Protestant take-over of their land.

After the failure of James II's come-back, William tried to treat Irish Catholics fairly. But in 1691 Ireland's Parliament, which was dominated by Protestants, passed a series of laws which deprived Irish Catholics of nearly all their rights. These injustices have never been forgotten or forgiven. They are remembered in the conflict between Northern Irish Protestants and Catholics which continues today.

▶ *Damage caused by an IRA bomb in modern-day Ireland.*

▼ *The Battle of the Boyne – 1690.*

When Mary was first told that she was to marry her cousin, William, she cried for a day and a half. Yet, in spite of this, the marriage was happy and when Mary died, William was heartbroken.

From 1689 until Mary's death in 1694, William and his wife ruled jointly. William then ruled alone until his own death eight years later.

During this period a number of extremely important laws were passed. Together they stated that all Protestants should be allowed to worship as they wished; that all future monarchs had to be members of the Protestant Church of England; that Parliament should be summoned every three years; and that no monarch could have an army, raise taxes or cancel laws without Parliament's consent. These last changes gave Parliament more control over the nation than it had had at the start of the Stuart era. They also helped to pave the way for the type of government that many countries have today.

WILLIAM'S WAR

William's main aim in life was to stop the Catholic French taking over Europe. So one of the first things he did after his coronation was drag England into war with France. Many people approved of this war and followed their new king into battle willingly. Others, however, saw it as a Dutch affair and resented being involved.

William's devotion to Holland and all things Dutch eventually made him unpopular, and when he died in 1702, few of his subjects were sorry to see him go.

THE AGE OF ANNE

MARLBOROUGH'S WAR

William's war against the French ended in 1697, but the peace did not last long. In 1700 Carlos II of Spain died, leaving his entire empire to the French. Needless to say, the rest of Europe were not happy about this, and by 1702 Holland, Britain and Austria were once again at war with France.

This war, known as the War of the Spanish Succession, lasted until 1713. Under the leadership of John Churchill, Duke of Marlborough, the English won four great battles. Together, these victories secured more colonies for England and helped to make her a major European power.

▼ *Blenheim Palace in Oxfordshire was given to John Churchill by Queen Anne as a reward for his victory at the Battle of Blenheim in 1704.*

FROM JAMES TO ANNE

The War of the Spanish Succession coincided almost exactly with the reign of the last Stuart monarch, Queen Anne. Anne was the second daughter of James II. When William III died without an heir, she inherited the throne and reigned until her own death in 1714.

By the end of Anne's reign England was much more prosperous than under James I. The country's mining and shipbuilding industries were more developed and overseas trade was more profitable. By 1714 English merchants not only had busy trade links with the Far East, but also with Britain's own colonies which now included parts of Canada, India, the West Indies, and most of North America's east coast. These trading ties brought luxury goods such as sugar, tobacco, tea, coffee, chocolate, silks and spices flooding into the country. Many of these goods were then sold to Europe at a great profit.

RICH TEA

Although the new luxury foods were in great demand by the rich, most people could not afford them. Instead they had to make do with their usual diet of mostly bread, beer and cheese. If an ordinary person wanted to enjoy a cup of tea they would probably have had to part with a week's wages first!

▲ The arrival of coffee in England led to the opening of coffee houses, where fashionable gentlemen could go to chat, smoke, and read newspapers. The first daily newspaper, The Daily Courant, was published in 1702 and it soon became popular with the coffee house crowds.

A KING CALLED GEORGE

Stout and prone to gout, Queen Anne had an unhappy life. None of her 18 children lived for very long, and when she herself died in 1714, the Stuart monarchy died with her.

After Anne's death, her throne passed to George of Hanover, a Protestant German relative of James I. George and his family were not very imaginative when it came to choosing christian names. So for the next hundred years Britain was ruled by a succession of kings all called George! Not surprisingly, this period is often referred to as the Georgian Age.

◀ Many of the luxury goods from Britain's colonies were produced by West African slaves.

29

GLOSSARY

Accession – a coming to office (for example, James I's accession to the throne).

Architect – someone who designs buildings.

Astronomy – the study of stars and planets.

Catholic (Roman Catholic) – a Christian who belongs to the Catholic Church which is headed by the Pope in Rome.

Conspiracy – a plot.

Dictator – an all-powerful ruler. A military dictator rules with the support of the army.

Empire – a wide-spread group of lands ruled by one powerful country.

Ermine – the white fur of a stoat with the black tail-tip attached.

Extremist – someone who holds strong, firm opinions.

Gout – a disease which causes swelling, especially of the big toe.

Gravity – the force that holds us on the ground and stops us floating off into space.

Marionette – a puppet moved by strings.

Middle Ages – the period of history from about the 700s to 1500 A.D.

Monarch – a king or queen.

Monarchy – a government headed by a king or queen.

Parliamentarian – someone who supports parliament or is skilled in the ways of parliament.

Physics – a type of science.

Protestant – a Christian who protested against the Roman Catholic Church in the 1500s.

Puritan – nickname given to someone who wanted to "purify" the Protestant Church of England and get rid of all traces of Catholicism. Puritans first began to emerge during Elizabeth I's reign.

Restoration – a return to kingship.

Sewage – refuse such as dirty water and urine which is carried in underground pipes, or sewers, to a sewage works. In Stuart times, there were no drain pipes or sewers so everyone just threw their dirty washing water etc. into the street.

Tenant – someone who rents their home or farm.

Transatlantic – crossing the Atlantic Ocean.

RESOURCES

PLACES TO VISIT

Cromwell Museum
Grammar School Walk,
Huntingdon, Cambridgeshire
Tel: 0480 425830

The Cromwell Museum illustrates the life of Oliver Cromwell, and the Parliamentary side of the Puritan revolution of 1642-1660.

The Museum of London
London Wall
London EC2Y 5HN
Tel: 071 600 3699

The Museum of London has a good collection of Tudor and Stuart artefacts and a children's activity room which is open during the school holidays.

Oakwell Hall Country Park
Nutter Lane
Birstall
Batley
Yorkshire.
Tel: 0924 474926.

This 16th century manor house has been furnished with a mixture of contemporary and reproduction late 17th century furniture. Other attractions/facilities include period gardens, an adventure playground and nature trail.

The Old House
High Town
Hereford
Tel: 0432 268121 ext 207

This house is preserved as a Jacobean period museum.

The Shakespeare Globe Museum and the Rose Theatre Exhibition
Bear Gardens
London SE1.
Tel: 071 928 6342.

The museum houses a permanent exhibition covering the history of London theatre from 1576-1642.

The Tower of London
Tower Hill
London EC3N 4AB
Tel: 071 709 0765

This mediaeval fortress houses all sorts of historic artefacts, including the Crown Jewels.